Original title:
Orchids of Elegy

Copyright © 2025 Creative Arts Management OÜ
All rights reserved.

Author: Dorian Ashford
ISBN HARDBACK: 978-1-80566-614-1
ISBN PAPERBACK: 978-1-80566-899-2

Soft Hues of Heartache

Petals weep in pastel tones,
Balloons float, but then they moan.
Witty whispers in the breeze,
Fading like old buttered cheese.

Laughter dances with the gloom,
In the garden, life finds room.
With every smile that falls apart,
A giggle stitches up the heart.

Swaying branches, clumsy bees,
Twisted love caught in the trees.
Dresses rustle, hiccups play,
In the sun, it's a grand ballet.

So here's to love, like silly clowns,
Falling hard in mismatched gowns.
From heartache blooms a jest too bright,
Underneath the faint moonlight.

Nightshade and Daydreams

In shadows of the night we tease,
Dreams hang low like bumblebees.
A giggle here, a chuckle there,
Frolics fill the midnight air.

Dancing mice with tiny hats,
Whisper secrets to the bats.
Each nightshade sip brings endless cheer,
"Cheers!" we shout, "But no more beer!"

Frogs in suits spin tales of love,
While crickets strum as stars above.
Caught in yearning, we all sway,
A merry dance till break of day.

So raise your cup to moonlit schemes,
As we toast to our wacky dreams.
In shades of night where laughter sings,
We find the joy that madness brings.

Floral Soliloquy

Petals speak in whispers calm,
With giggles wrapped in nature's charm.
Here comes a daisy, dressed in white,
Reciting jokes until the night.

A rose rolls eyes, with pranks in store,
While poppies snicker from the floor.
Each bloom plays tricks, oh what a sight,
Floral laughter takes to flight.

Leaves take turns to tell their tale,
From silly falls to epic fail.
In this garden of glee and fun,
Each bloom shines brightly, one by one.

So join the party, don't be shy,
The flowers laugh, oh me, oh my!
In every petal, humor flows,
A comedy where friendship grows.

Remembrance in Bloom

Forgotten thoughts in vibrant hues,
We reminisce of wacky views.
With every laugh that fades to sigh,
A memory blooms, oh me, oh my.

Here lies a flower with a frown,
Yet tells the world not to back down.
A weedy tale of love's regret,
Blooms alongside all we forget.

Laughter lingers in the air,
As happy moments disappear.
Each petal holds a laugh once shared,
In this garden, nothing's ensnared.

So plant your smiles, make them grow,
In fields where past and present flow.
A joyful jest, a poignant tune,
In every bloom, the heart finds room.

Ghosts Among the Vines

In the garden where shadows play,
Ghosts whisper jokes in a cheeky way.
They lift weights made of chives and thyme,
With clumsy grace, they dance in rhyme.

They trip on roots, the silly things,
Wearing daisies as tiny rings.
Each chuckle echoes through the leaves,
As laughter blooms where humor weaves.

Lament of the Petal's Caress

A petal sighed, it missed the bees,
Who preferred buzzing 'round their knees.
With every flounce and every sway,
It tried to lure them with ballet.

But oh! The bee was quite a tease,
"Your dance is sweet, but not my breeze!"
So petals fell, in tragic pose,
Constructing crowns from the fallen rose.

Fragile Echoes of Grace

In delicate sighs, the petals sway,
Trying to charm the bumblebee's day.
But whispers turn to boisterous shouts,
As they forget what elegance is about.

With wobbly stems, they feign a bow,
Spilling pollen, oh! Look at them now!
Grace is lost in each clumsy dive,
Yet laughter blooms, oh what a vibe!

Dancer Beneath the Moonlight

A flower spun beneath the moon,
Tripped on a root, played a tune.
With petals flapping, it leaped in bliss,
How funny to see such a flowery miss!

The night air giggled, "What a sight!"
As the dancer twirled, nearly took flight.
But laughter reigned, not grace or fear,
For humor blooms when flowers veer.

Mourning in Full Bloom

In the garden where laughter weeps,
A plant in a pot takes its leap.
With petals like giggles, it sways and bends,
As neighbors all whisper, 'Just make amends!'

The daisies chuckle, they know it's true,
The roses turn red, but they don't feel blue.
In this floral parade with mascara and cheer,
The sunflowers shout, "Don't shed a tear!"

Botanical Memories

Snapshots of petals in quirky frames,
Lettuce recalls all the vegetable games.
With hearts made of chlorophyll just in case,
They reminisce of a tomato's embrace.

The snapdragons grin, and the lilacs applaud,
While ferns do the cha-cha, pretending they trod.
In this memory lane of botanical zest,
Every bloom is a jester at nature's wild fest.

Exhale of a Dying Flower

A flower sneezes, pollen takes flight,
It's a dramatic end, what a comical sight!
With petals sagging like old karaoke stars,
It whispers, "I'm tired, let's save up the bars."

And daisies just wink, with a nod from the rose,
Everyone knows how the drama just grows.
With laughter and sighs, they dance in decay,
"Let's eulogize fun, in our own silly way!"

The Past in Petal Form

Petals unfold tales of laughter and glee,
Of bees sneezing loudly with wild jubilee.
As petals recall every garden affair,
They roll on the ground—in a bloomin' flair!

The violets gossip, the tulips all sigh,
While the lilies proclaim they could surely fly.
Blast from the bloom brings a chuckle on cue,
For every flower dreams of a past so true!

Transient Beauty

In a garden bright, they strut and sway,
Petals tickle bees, come out to play.
Their colors shout, a riotous song,
But fade too fast, where do they belong?

Dancing on stems, a comical show,
One slight breeze, and down they go!
They giggle in the sun, then quickly frown,
Catching a cold when the sun goes down!

Beneath the Withering Canopy

Under leaves thick, they take a nap,
Dreaming of rainbows, or a witty clap.
With every sigh, a petal drops,
Who knew beauty ends in such funny flops?

Waving hello to the curious bugs,
Sending them packing, with a polite shrug.
In their prime, they twirl and swirl,
Then turn to a joke with every twirl!

Ode to the Silent Growth

In shadowed corners, they stretch and yawn,
With silent giggles, they greet the dawn.
Reaching for sunshine, they twist and bend,
Pretending they're small, the fun never ends!

A sly little smile, they play hard to get,
All while they plot a quirky duet.
With roots in the muck, they aim for the sky,
The tallest joke with a shy little sigh.

Forgotten Elegance

Once grand and proud, they sit in a vase,
Now telling tales with a funny face.
Used to be stars in the floral parade,
Now whispering secrets that surely evade.

Dust gathers softly, like laughter's delight,
Poking their petals in the quiet night.
They reminisce about days so bold,
When they danced for the sun, a story retold!

Veil of Scented Tears

In a garden lush and green,
Laughed a flower with a sheen.
Once it wilting, wore a frown,
'Why do I look like a clown?'

Nature's jest, so sly and sweet,
Rained down petals, a flowing sheet.
For every tear dropped down the soil,
A hearty chuckle in the toil.

Bumblebees with buzz so loud,
Vacuuming nectar, oh so proud.
But in the breeze, they'd dance their lanes,
Tickling blossoms, exchanging gains.

So here's to blooms that weep and grin,
Embracing chaos, life's wild spin.
In giggles masked, in fragrant cheer,
We celebrate each flowing tear.

The Tranquil Mourner

In the shadows, a soft sigh,
A plant or two begins to cry.
'Why so sad?' a leaf inquires,
'Join the dance, ignite the fires!'

Petals brushed with laughter's hue,
Comfy sofas, a faux pas view.
A bud whispers, 'Let's have fun!'
While jokers on the branch all run.

Every droop and every bend,
Hints that mourning can just blend.
"I'll wear a hat," the stem declares,
"But only if we do it bare!"

So sadness takes its bow tonight,
As blossoms twirl with sheer delight.
The tranquil mourners laugh instead,
With smiles fluffed where tears once bled.

Faded Petal Memories

Once vibrant blooms with tales to tell,
Now sit in corners, lost in spell.
'What happened to those days of cheer?'
'Let's reminisce, let's bring them near!'

A faded petal lifts its face,
'Who knew a wilt could hold such grace?'
And bending leaves with gentle flair,
Shout, 'We're still fabulous, don't you dare!'

In dusty air, a giggle rang,
'Oh look, it's that flower who sang!'
Memories drift like whiffs of joy,
Every snap and laugh, then they destroy.

And here we pause, in sighs and jest,
With petals crumbling, still the best.
For in each fold, a story's spun,
Life's blooms wilt, but never shun.

Threads of Grief

In tangled vines, they weave and spin,
Threads of laughter, where to begin?
'Pull along,' the roots have said,
'If we trip, let's laugh instead!'

A gardener plucks a leaf forlorn,
'This one's gloomy; let's not scorn!'
With stitches bright, they patch with ease,
Grief becomes a perfect tease.

Sunlight trickles through the shade,
Helping blooms to unafraid.
'Stop crying now,' a blossom grinned,
'Life's too short to let it end!'

So gather round, all petal friends,
As every tear like laughter blends.
In threads of grief, let's sew our smiles,
And dance together across the miles.

The Soul Between the Petals

In the garden where giggles bloom,
Petals whisper secrets of doom.
A bee in a suit, takes a sip,
Winking at flowers with a flip.

A sun hat tipped, and dancing boots,
Underneath the moon, everyone hoots.
A daisy and rose in a funny debate,
Over who's taller and who's first-rate.

With laughter that flutters, they twist and twirl,
A worm tells a joke, and the daisies hurl.
"Why did the plant stay home today?"
"Too rooted, it said, for a wild ballet!"

The petals curl up with a chuckling grin,
As the night's antics begin to spin.
With echoes of fun, they dance in the breeze,
Creating a spectacle sure to please.

Blossoms of Reflection

In the mirror of dew, a flower is found,
Doing face-pulls and cartwheels around.
A tulip in tights flexes with glee,
While a rose strikes a pose, as fancy as she.

Reflections that giggle, a sight so absurd,
Where petals recite the latest birdword.
A lily attempts to compose a rhyme,
But trips on her stem, oh, what a crime!

The moonlight giggles, the stars seem to clap,
As daisies moonwalk and give a quick flap.
"Life's too short," shouts a bright marigold,
"Let's dance till we wilt, let's be brave, and bold!"

With laughter in spades, they bring in the night,
Blossoms of joy in a playful delight.
So, grab your own bloom and join in the cheer,
In this garden of giggles, come dance without fear!

A Tapestry of Fading Colors

In gardens where colors dance,
Bumblebees forget to prance.
Petals whisper jokes so bold,
While sunlight's laughter turns to gold.

Leaves gossip by the breeze,
Wishing clouds would drop to knees.
Colors fade, but who's to care?
They're busy combing through their hair.

Violets plot a sneaky heist,
Stealing sunlight, oh so nice!
Daisies chuckle, 'What a mess!'
While tulips strut in fancy dress.

In this riot of fading light,
Nature's humor takes to flight.
A tapestry where hues collide,
In laughter, treasures we abide.

Twilight Reflections in Petals

As twilight blushes, colors bloom,
Petals laugh, dispelling gloom.
In the mirror of fading skies,
They wink and giggle, oh what spies!

A daffodil in a bowler hat,
Claims he's the king, just look at that!
Sunsets yawn, while shadows tease,
Echoing whispers in evening breeze.

Napping roses share a joke,
About the gardener's favorite smoke.
Underneath the stars so bright,
Petals disco, oh what a sight!

With each flicker of the night,
Fun in bloom, what pure delight!
As laughter spills on velvet floor,
Nature's jesters, we adore.

The Memory of Blooming Silence

In quiet corners, whispers play,
Petals share secrets day by day.
A blushing bud with tales of cheer,
Reports on bees that disappear!

Silence chuckles, tickles the air,
While dandelions plot with flair.
A shy bloom struts in solitude,
Sipping nectar, not in the mood.

Fading echoes of laughter swell,
With tales that nature loves to tell.
In silence, blooms pass notes of glee,
Can flowers giggle? Come and see!

A memory forged in petals bright,
Humming softly in the night.
While blooms may fade, their humor stays,
In whispered blooms, we find our ways.

Lush Silhouettes of the Past

In shadows deep where laughter dwells,
Silhouettes of blooms share their spells.
A fanciful waltz in the moon's attire,
   Petals dance like they're on fire.

The past is filled with colors bright,
Vines play tricks under the night.
With every swish, they tease the air,
'Who needs a vase? We're free, we swear!'

Lush whispers in the twilight haze,
Remind us of our carefree days.
Blooming memories skip and twirl,
   In a garden where ruckus unfurl.

With each silhouette, a story's spun,
In laughter's glow, they're never done.
Embrace the past with petals bold,
   In a world where humor's gold.

Unfurling Grief

In a garden where laughter grows,
Petals dance on toes of woes.
I watered feelings, let them bloom,
But now they're sprouting up in gloom.

With every sigh, the weeds come back,
While blossoms jest, I lose my track.
A flowered hat upon my head,
Is that my heart, or just the shed?

The flowers giggle, petals tease,
While I lament my fallen knees.
But bloopers of the plant parade,
Make me laugh, or I'm afraid.

So, I shall grow a garden bright,
Of silly blooms in sheer delight.
With every throb and mild dismay,
They cheer me on, they bloom and play.

The Weight of Silk

In velvet folds of humor's guise,
The petals sigh with flirty ties.
A draped lament of silky threads,
Wraps around my joking heads.

Each laughter's pang, a twinkling sprout,
Too awkward, like a danceabout.
As wilting petals drop like rain,
I'll prance and jest to hide the pain.

The colors swirl, a clumsy reel,
As feelings tug like tangled wheel.
With every slip, the laughter grows,
A tangled mess, where joy bestows.

So, in this garden of my plight,
I wear my woes with heart alight.
A silken veil, a funny plume,
In every bloom, I chase the gloom.

Nostalgic Flora

In memory's garden, roots entwine,
Where laughter meets a wistful vine.
I planted thoughts of yesteryears,
But now they sprout a mix of tears.

With every bud, a chuckle wakes,
Though wilted blooms can crack like flakes.
Their blossoms nod, and softly grin,
As I rehash where I've been.

I trim the stems of joy and doubt,
While silly dreams keep popping out.
The flowers nodding in delight,
Remind me of my quirky plight.

So let's parade through memory's lane,
With petals bright, and not a stain.
Let laughter guide this floral tour,
In echoes sweet and pure encore.

Last Light on Blossom Lane

As dusk descends on petals fair,
The giggles float upon the air.
A final bloom before the night,
In vibrant hues, it laughs in light.

The evening's dance, a playful breeze,
Twists joyous blooms, with wobbly knees.
Their colors clash, a comical fight,
In fading hues, they twirl in flight.

With every flutter, joy's refrain,
Brings forth a chuckle, sweet as rain.
The flowers wink, with mirthful glee,
In crooked lines, so wild and free.

So let this light turn grief to cheer,
As blossoms sway, they tease and leer.
In twilight's glow, they poke and play,
A plant-filled jest to end the day.

Whispers in the Bloom

In a garden dressed in cheer,
Petals giggle, loud and near.
A bee buzzed in with quite a flair,
Saying, 'I'm just here for the hair!'

The daisies tease, 'Oh, what a sight!'
While tulips declare, 'We own the night!'
The breeze tells jokes, oh so discreet,
And roses laugh, saying, 'Aren't we sweet?'

With colors bright, the garden quips,
A parroting parrot takes wild trips.
Each bloom in bloom, a secret told,
In this floral world, we're never old!

So let's dance on this fragrant stage,
Where flowers prance, like kids in a cage.
With every petal, a funny tune,
A wild fiesta under the moon!

Petals of the Past

In the attic, pots of green,
Remembering all the sights unseen.
With each sprout, a story grows,
Of raucous nights and garden shows.

A cactus grins with a prickly jest,
'Last week's blooms? Well, they were a pest!'
While violets reminisce in hues,
About the days they all wore shoes.

Lily pads laugh in a sunlit pond,
'What's that weird smell? Oh, be fond!'
And the ferns add in with a swoosh,
'What do you mean? We're all very lush!'

Together they giggle, a floral parade,
With whispers of laughter that won't soon fade.
Time drips slowly, but blooms never end,
In petals of past, we all make amends!

Silken Shadows of Remembrance

In the twilight's soft embrace,
Balloons of thoughts begin to race.
A moth flutters, in fancy dress,
'Excuse me, is this a floral mess?'

Petals sway under rumor's reign,
'You heard what Jasmine said about Jane?'
Daisies snicker, with a knowing look,
'Oh please, that one's in the wrong book!'

The shadows dance, a quirky lot,
While moonlight winks, and laughter's caught.
In the stillness, old jokes revive,
Each whispering petal, so sly, so alive!

With silk threads stitching memories bright,
We find the joy in the dimmest night.
So let's toast with dew from the grass,
To silken shadows that forever amass!

Elegance in Decay

Oh look, the petals start to fall,
But dare I say, they've had a ball!
With laughter echoing in the breeze,
'Time to shed our layers, if you please.'

The trunk creaks, a squeaky song,
'This isn't just decay, it feels so strong!'
The leaves exchange their jokes with ease,
'Who knew being wilted could feel like a tease?'

In the final act, the colors fade,
Yet still they twirl, a grand parade.
For with every petal that drifts away,
There's still a spark in the bright array!

So raise a glass to those who go,
For elegance dances, even slow.
In every ending, there's humor, you see,
A glorious jest in this grand jubilee!

Fragrant Sorrows Unfold

In the garden where giggles bloom,
Petals whisper secrets in the room,
With a sigh and a chuckle they grow,
Tales of love that no one will know.

When the sunshine tickles their face,
They dance in a most peculiar grace,
Beneath the weight of bouncing bees,
Lost in a world of floral joys and tease.

Each drooping bud wears a frown,
Yet still manages to twirl around,
A misfit laugh behind a leaf,
Blossoms share their tales of grief.

Petal parties where few would dare,
With pollen confetti flying in the air,
Laughter mingling with fragrant despair,
Such is the life of beauties rare.

The Language of Fallen Stems

In silence, each stem begins to speak,
Awkwardly funny, with a twist and a peek,
Whispers of love that fell from the sky,
Giggling roots that know how to lie.

The blooms recall their glorious days,
When they were the stars in sun's warm rays,
Now they chuckle at their twisty fate,
Dancing lightly, not tempting the date.

Every fallen petal holds a jest,
Life is a farce in this floral fest,
Cacti snicker at their velvet friends,
As evenings descend and laughter blends.

In this garden where humor grows tall,
Each wobbly stem recalls its own fall,
With every chuckle comes a bright gleam,
A silly tale woven into a dream.

Ethereal Beauty in Twilight

As the sun dips low with a wink,
Petals plan mischief, but can't quite think,
They flutter about with giggly glee,
Chasing shadows, wild and free.

At twilight's call, they play hide and seek,
With moonlight wrapping them, soft and sleek,
Tales of blunders fill the air,
Fragrant laughter, everywhere.

In the hush of night, blooms come alive,
Swaying gently, as if to strive,
For the title of the night's best prank,
Glancing shyly at the riverbank.

Each fragrant sigh a comical glance,
Beneath the stars, they frolic and dance,
For beauty, it seems, knows how to jest,
In the hidden twilight, they are truly blessed.

Secret Gardens of Forgotten Loves

In the secret nooks where old things sigh,
Faded love stories dance and fly,
Petals in ruffles tell tales of old,
In whispers of laughter, their secrets unfold.

Where the sun once kissed each charming face,
Now giggles echo, filling the space,
Misadventures bloom in playful hues,
With tangled vines and colorful cues.

Each bud, a flicker of a past delight,
Winks at the moon in the cool of the night,
With every crinkle, a cheeky smile,
Love was once grand, but now it's a while.

In corners where memories softly nap,
Life's little hiccups form a comedic map,
Lost fragrances in a world so jovial,
In gardens hidden, love remains historical.

Velvet Shadows

In corners dark where petals shrink,
The flowers plot, or so we think.
They tiptoe 'round in silent glee,
A sneaky crew of botanical spree.

With whispers light, they share their jokes,
The stems all shake, the leaves provoke.
They giggle soft, oh what a sight,
In velvet shadows, they dance at night.

Each bloom a chortle, each root a pun,
They weave their tales, oh what fun!
They toast to moths on fancy nights,
In petal tops and leafy flights.

Yet, when we glance, they quickly freeze,
Pretending to be just a tease.
But in that hush, a wink remains,
For laughter blooms, despite the claims.

In the Garden of Remembrance

In this sweet plot, where memories grow,
The daisies chuckle, putting on a show.
With rhubarb hats and minty ties,
They spin their tales beneath the skies.

A daisied dog sings off-key,
As lilacs laugh from their tall spree.
The veggies gossip, sprouting tall,
In silly whispers, they heed the call.

They tell of love and clumsy bees,
Of sunlit days and joyful breeze.
The squashes don't mind, they grin so wide,
In this bright garden, they take great pride.

But evening falls, they know the drill,
They tuck themselves, quiet and still.
Yet 'neath the stars, their laughter rings,
In memories sweet, where joy still clings.

Echoes of Delicate Fragrance

In twilight's glow, the scents collide,
With floral grins, they can't abide.
They dance around in fragrant flights,
Cheering blooms with funny sights.

A jasmine twirls with mismatched shoes,
While lilies laugh at all the blues.
With rosy puns that float so far,
They puff up pride like a tiny star.

The violets snicker in shadows deep,
As scents take turns, a fragrant leap.
With breath of mint, they mock the sage,
In this great play, they take the stage.

Yet when we wander near their show,
They feign a fade, a dance so slow.
But drift away, you'll catch them near,
In echoes soft, their humor clear.

Sylvan Lament

In stately woods where trees may weep,
The flowers sigh, their secrets keep.
With roots entwined in whispered tales,
They sport their woes like silly veils.

A dandelion cracks a joke,
While weary ferns begin to choke.
"Why so glum?" the daisies cry,
"Just spread your seeds and let them fly!"

The willows sway, they mime a dance,
"Life's just a jig, so take a chance!"
Their laughter drifts on woodland air,
As shadows blend with evening's stare.

Yet when the moon takes up its cue,
They still their games, as night blooms too.
But still within the night's embrace,
A gentle joy finds every place.

Eclipsed by Grace

In the garden, blooms so fine,
The neighbor thinks they're all divine.
But look a bit closer, you'll surely find,
They've got a knack for mischief, oh so unkind.

With petals flapping like a silly hat,
They sway and tease, imagine that!
A dance-off soon, but who'll take the prize?
A flower with attitude wins in disguise.

What elegance hides in each little stem,
Yet pollen's like glitter, causing mayhem.
They're whispering jokes while I roll my eyes,
Oh flowers, you jest while the whole world complies.

So here's to the blooms that love a good laugh,
In their garden silly, they carve out their path.
With grace they eclipse all who's half-hearted,
But beware of the gardener, the dance has just started.

The Scent of Longing

Love in the air, or is it just me?
The flowers keep laughing, can't wait to see!
They bloom with a wink and giggles abound,
As if they're all plotting, secretly wound.

A whiff of romance, it's all just a game,
The fragrances clash in a whimsical frame.
What's that I smell? A hint of surprise,
These blossoms conspire with crafty disguise.

With buds in a chatter, they stir up the feels,
Their perfumed ambitions give all the appeals.
Each whispering petal is light and bright,
Yet they grin mischievously, day turns to night.

So here's to the scent that dances and sways,
Where longing is cheeky and often decays.
They'll lure and they'll tease, but beware the charms,
For blooms can be rascals with fanciful arms.

Echoing Colors

In hues so bright, they paint the scene,
Laughing at faces that go unseen.
A rainbow of petals, they shout with glee,
As I trip on roots, oh, look at me!

Each color a jest in nature's remark,
Roses get shy, but the daisies embark.
With lilac giggles and tulip tones,
It's a carnival here in the flower zones.

They whisper sweet nothings in shades of delight,
But when you bend down, it's a floral fright!
A paint splatter party, a joke on the breeze,
Petal confetti? Oh, don't mind the tease!

So here's to the colors that echo and play,
In gardens where laughter refuses to sway.
With nature's laughter, forever it grows,
In fields where the cheeky excitement just flows.

Serene Farewells

With a slow bow they take their last glance,
Twirling around in a farewell dance.
Plants chuckle softly as night steals the light,
How fitting they leave in a whimsical sight.

Petals afloat like they're floating on air,
Making quick quips as if they don't care.
No tears in the garden, just giggles at bay,
Serene little poise—what a funny bouquet!

As dusk draws near, they grumble and sigh,
"Don't let us go, we're too bright to die!"
Yet still they curl up in a playful embrace,
In slumber they snicker, oh what a grace.

So here's to farewells that dance and delight,
In the heart of the evening, what a beautiful sight.
With humor entwined in their soft, gentle sway,
They bid us goodbye in the silliest way.

Rituals of the Flowering Heart

A flower in a pot sings soft tunes,
Like a grandma gossiping 'round noon.
Her petals wave with comedic flair,
While bees dance as if they haven't a care.

Bumbling blooms in mismatched clothes,
One petal's loud, the other just doze.
They giggle when the sun starts to rise,
And whisper secrets to butterflies.

In the garden, a dance-off begins,
With daisies laughing, waving their fins.
Tulips try to spin, but end up a flop,
While roses say, 'You're all gonna stop!'

At dusk, the flowers tell a joke,
A cactus slips on dew, oh what a poke.
Under the stars, the petals unite,
With a chuckle, they embrace the night.

Revered Remnants

In the vase, a wilted bloom attempts,
To tell a story of floral pretense.
'Remember when I was the life of the ball?'
Now I mumble to petals trying to stand tall.

The fridge attracts the scent of regret,
Leftover blooms, far from a pet vet.
They reminisce about the days of sun,
Now it's all droopy, with laughter undone.

A leaf confesses it once twirled with flair,
Till a strong wind declared, 'Life's not fair!'
They giggle 'til they cry, what a mess,
In the garden of life, we sure are blessed.

Dust gathers like laughter, we keep it alive,
In the compost pile, where memories thrive.
With jokes from the soil and giggles with air,
The remnants stay revered, if even a hair.

Flowers in the Stillness

In the moment of stillness, flowers conspire,
To plan a heist to steal back their fire.
They plot silly pranks with petals to trade,
A daisy once danced, now all out of grade.

Tulips whisper sweet nothings to bees,
'Oh, give us a break! Can't you see we're at ease?'
But buzzing progresses, and petals chime in,
In this garden of mischief, it's all in good spin.

The sun giggles down, oh what a sight,
As flowers try stand-up under moonlight.
A poppy tells jokes about the weeds' bad hair,
While violets snicker, 'Not us, we're rare!'

In the stillness, the laughter grows loud,
Peeking through petals, a giggling crowd.
In the quiet of evening, the secrets unfold,
Flowers in stillness, sharing tales bold.

Petals to Remember

Gather 'round, petals, it's time for a chat,
Tales of a squirrel and his mischiefy hat.
The daisies giggle, the lilies just sigh,
While the rose rolls its eyes, 'Oh, how they do fly!'

They share with a laugh how the wind likes to tease,
A bouquet in the breeze sways with such ease.
Watch out for bees—they dance with a sting,
In the petals' perspective, it's a wonderful thing.

Together they plot to grow really tall,
Just to audition for a flower ball.
With sequins of dew and petals of cheer,
They'll waltz through the seasons, spreading good cheer.

So here's to the blooms, the laughter, the fun,
Every petal remembers the joy under sun.
In the garden of life, wear your petals proud,
For the laughter of flowers is always allowed.

When Flowers Weep in Starlight

In the garden, flowers sigh,
Crying petals, oh so spry.
They spill their dew like laughter bright,
Underneath the moon's soft light.

A daisy cracked a funny joke,
While tulips giggled, nearly broke.
A weeping willow heard the blare,
And danced like no one had a care.

The roses wrapped in velvet grace,
Stumbled on their own embrace.
"Is that a bee, or just my fate?"
They whispered with a cheeky gait.

As starlight drips like honeyed wine,
The blooms connect, their laughter twine.
With tears, they paint a silly night,
Where joy and sorrow dance in flight.

Shadows of Blooming Absence

A shadow speaks, a petal's woe,
"Where's that flower? Don't you know?"
The sun's too bright, the breeze too brisk,
They ponder blooms in a smoky whisk.

"Did he run off for a sweet tea?"
Said a sunflower, cringing with glee.
"Or perhaps he's off to see a show,
While we're here basking in the glow!"

A crumpled leaf, with tales to tell,
Grumbled softly, "What the hell?"
"Must be nice to have a dance,
While we're left here in TF dance!"

But despite their absent bud's charms,
They threw a party in the arms.
They laughed and spun in empty air,
Blooming joy without a care.

Whispers of Petals

Petals whisper secrets low,
In a language only blooms may know.
"Did you hear about that bee?"
"He's quite the flirt, oh don't you see!"

A violet blushed, her color bright,
"We've got gossip shock tonight!"
While lilies rolled their leafy eyes,
At tales of clumsy, love-struck flies.

"What's that smell? A rotten bud?"
"Oh, dear petals, what a dud!"
They chuckled softly, petals flung,
As petals danced, their hearts were sung.

On this breeze of banter light,
They twirled beneath the starry height.
For even in whispers of despair,
They found laughter blooming in the air.

The Mourning Blooms

In a pot of dim despair,
A daisy donned a somber air.
"Oh dear, my friend, how could you go?"
The tulips sighed, their heads hung low.

"Is it the pot or just bad luck?"
Chortled a bloom as he plucked.
"If we could dance like weeds, you see,
We'd have more fun, just wait for me!"

A rose declared, "With sadness rife,
We'll celebrate your garden life!"
And threw a bash with wilted flair,
Where flowers lamented without a care.

"Let's toast to petals lost in dreams,
For they shall bloom in silly schemes."
The night, it filled with joyous cheer,
As laughter rang, the shadows clear.

Veils of Silence

In the garden where whispers dwell,
Petals gossip, oh so swell.
A butterfly flirts with a bee,
Is nature throwing a big tea spree?

Colors clash in a dance so bright,
Who knew flowers could be such a sight?
With stalks so proud, they twist and bend,
A mishap waiting on the garden's trend.

In moments still, the bees do buzz,
While blooms pretend to speak, just because.
"Did you hear about last night's bloom?"
"They outshone the roses, what a gloom!"

So here's to gardens and their giggle,
Where even daisies can make us wiggle.
In every petal's soft embrace,
Laughter blooms, a flowery race.

Nature's Eulogy

Upon a hill, the daisies lament,
With such flair, they are heaven-sent.
"Who's the fairest in the patch?"
"Stay tuned, darling, it's quite the match!"

The trees sigh, with leaves that flutter,
As squirrels gather over the last peanut butter.
"Is that a tear in the willow's eye?"
"Nope, just rain, darling, oh my!"

A crow caws with a jester's tone,
"Why so serious? You're not alone!"
The lupines laugh, in silken threads,
While dandelions bloom like unmade beds.

In every shade of green or gold,
Nature shows us tales untold.
With winks and whispers, it carries on,
A eulogy penned with a cheeky yawn.

Elegy of the Wildflower

A wildflower stands, bold and free,
Wrapped in stories of you and me.
"Why so shy?" asks a grand old tree,
"Let's dance like it's a jubilee!"

With roots that dig and stems that sway,
They chuckle at petals that won't obey.
"It's not a contest, just a show,"
"Unless you've got that rosé glow."

Bees in tuxedos rush and hum,
While ladybugs groove, oh what fun!
With scents so sweet, they call and tease,
"Join the party, if you please!"

So lift your blooms, let laughter sprout,
The wildflower's tale isn't filled with doubt.
In nature's whimsy, joy is found,
When petals waltz above the ground.

The Fragility of Farewell

Petals fall with a giggling toss,
Say goodbye, but not at a loss.
"Who knew goodbyes could be so spry?"
"Let's make it a party, oh my!"

Leaves sway softly, a tender embrace,
As nature chuckles in this space.
"Farewell to the sun, but what a show!"
"It's a blooming farewell, in case you didn't know!"

The daisies wink with a colorful flair,
While violets whisper without a care.
"Do you hear the trumpet of the breeze?"
"It's just the wind, bringing us ease!"

So here's to farewells, funny and bright,
A dance in dusk, a sparkling night.
In every goodbye from earth to sky,
Life's just a giggle, a reason to fly.

A Bloom for the Fallen

In gardens lush with colors bright,
A flower fell in the dead of night.
With petals soft and humor snide,
It whispered laughs, though death had tried.

The wind it danced, a cheeky tease,
Swaying low with whispered ease.
"You can't keep me down, not this bloom!"
It chuckled loud, filling the gloom.

From cornered cracks, it makes a stand,
A brave little laugh in a dreary land.
For every tear that falls like rain,
There's humor found in the mundane.

So cheers to blooms that won't conform,
In life's odd tragedy, they'll transform.
With every sigh from beneath the sun,
There's always a punchline to be spun.

Silent Reverie

In a quiet nook, a petal sighed,
Dressed in hues that mischief spied.
A thought it dreamed, quite out of tune,
That flowers danced beneath the moon.

With every sway, it cracked a grin,
For who would know where laughs begin?
In shadows cast by evening's grace,
It practiced jokes in a secret place.

Each whispered cheer brought forth delight,
As petals twirled in the soft moonlight.
A giggle here, a chuckle there,
In fields of dreams, naught a care.

So let the night hold tales untold,
Of flowers bold and laughter rolled.
In silent reveries, they take heart,
Turning sadness into art.

Petal-Crowned Sorrows

A crown of petals on a frowning face,
Wore sadness with quite a lot of grace.
"I tried to bloom, but who knew?"
It pondered deep with a touch of blue.

"I'll throw a party! Call the bees!"
It giggled loud, shook off the freeze.
With nectar sweet and joy in mind,
It planned a bash, good times to find.

With haphazard dance and silly feats,
It spun around on little feet.
For in the sorrow, laughter lay,
A merry heart will find its way.

So let your petals crown the pain,
And dance with glee in the summer rain.
In every frown, there's joy in store,
The petal crown forevermore.

The Last Breath of Spring

As spring waved bye with a sneaky wink,
A petal giggled, began to think.
"Will winter prevail? Can cold win out?"
On playful whispers it chose to shout.

With tiny breaths of fragrant cheer,
It draped the world with laughter near.
In every fold and sunny ray,
The last breath laughed before the gray.

"I'll float away like a feather bright,
Tickle the clouds, give them a fright!"
With every breeze that blew so sweet,
It found a rhythm, a quirky beat.

So as spring fades, let humor cling,
To each soft farewell it may bring.
For in the sigh of nature's end,
A flower's wit will always mend.

Echoes in the Dew

In the morning mist, they giggle,
Blushing petals start to wiggle.
Sipping sunlight, oh what a treat,
Dewy laughter at their feet.

With whispers soft of tales untold,
Bold colors dance, both bright and bold.
They jest at bees who come to sip,
While sipping nectar with a flip.

A butterfly stops, with wings so bright,
Stumbles 'round, much to their delight.
They point and jest with cheeky glee,
"More nectar, please! It's all for me!"

Their playful blooms in whimsical light,
Cheeky pranks till the fall of night.
With every rustle, they tease and sigh,
These clowns of nature, oh my, oh my!

Midnight Elegance in Fragrance

Under the moon, they pose and pout,
Glamorous blooms, there's never a doubt.
With perfume rich, they steal the show,
Who needs a lamp? Just watch them glow!

The stars roll their eyes, a jealous lot,
As flowers flex in their nightly plot.
"Why bother with sleep? We'll dance instead,"
A fragrance-filled party, dreams in their head.

Charming vines twist in playful cheer,
"Is that a moth? Quick, disappear!"
With laughter soft, they sway in time,
Creating chaos, doing what's prime.

A giggle here, a fragrance there,
In the garden, fun hangs in the air.
They keep the night alive with glee,
Midnight mischief, wild as can be!

Curses on the Orchid Breeze

A breeze so sweet, but oh so sly,
Stirred the petals, caught them awry.
"Who's been whispering, causing this mess?"
"Not me," they chime, "please, do confess!"

With laughter ringing all around,
A flower's vendetta knows no bound.
"Next time, dear breeze, don't play so bold,
Or you'll find us wedged in the cold!"

They plot and scheme with petals a-flare,
A fragrant revenge fills the air.
"Wrap them in ribbons, the breeze will rue!
Let's teach him once, just what we can do!"

Amidst bouquet mayhem, laughter unfurls,
Heed the whispers of these floral girls.
Cursed to sway in a breeze of fun,
These prankster buds are never done!

The Remnants of Silent Seasons

In echoes soft, the seasons play,
Where blooms once bright have lost their way.
With petals strewn in whimsical cheer,
They grumble, "Seasons, why can't you stay near?"

Once vibrant hues, so bold, now fade,
Bloomers complain in this charade.
"Spring was fine, but where's the sun?
The silence lingers, who's having fun?"

With garbled tales of what has passed,
These remnants wonder, will spring break fast?
"Ah, look! A bud!" they squeal with glee,
"Perhaps next year, it's us you'll see!"

So here they sit, in a dance of pause,
Amidst memories, laughter gives them cause.
In whispered giggles, a lesson they learn,
That every silence can take a turn!

Twilight's Floral Farewell

In gardens where odd blooms parade,
A daisy giggles, and a rose is afraid.
The violets chuckle, a bit out of place,
While tulips all blushing, try to keep pace.

The moon cracks jokes, as the petals all sway,
"Why do flowers never play hide-and-seek?" they say.
"Because they're too rooted, don't travel at all,
Except when a vase comes to make them feel small!"

As twilight draws near, the sun starts to yawn,
The lilies regale tales of dew at dawn.
Each blossom's a comedian, ready to bloom,
In the face of their fate, they dispel all the gloom.

With laughter in colors, a whimsical scene,
They bid their goodnight, not one single tear glean.
In a world full of petals, they dance in the air,
A floral farewell with a chuckle to share.

Gossamer Grief

In the orchard of quirks, where the petals all giggle,
The wisteria wobbles and tries not to wiggle.
The winds tell odd stories of bygone cheer,
While daisies retort, "We don't shed a tear!"

Mirth swirls in the breeze, the pansies invade,
"Why's everyone crying? We're all just being played!"
The hydrangeas whisper their secrets so sweet,
While peonies blush at the joke from a beet.

In each little corner, where flowers just jive,
Laughter erupts as they try to survive.
"Why so serious, dear friends?" a sunflower beams,
"When life gives you petals, just dance in your dreams!"

So gossamer grief hangs on petals so light,
With a smirk and a smile, they embrace the night.
As shadows grow long, they curl up in delight,
Resting on laughter, till morning's first light.

Fragile Whispers of Goodbye

In a meadow of merriment, the flowers convene,
A daffodil chuckles at a little green bean.
"Why are we here?" the violets declare,
"Is it too early for a fanciful fair?"

The lilacs are laughing, their jokes take flight,
As the lilies giggle at creeping twilight.
"Why don't flowers ever go for a swim?"
"Because with such roots, it's quite hard to begin!"

With fragile whispers amidst petals so bright,
They decide that goodbyes won't tarnish their night.
Instead of a frown, they choose to embrace,
Every fleeting moment, each delicate grace.

So the flora united, in jest near the sky,
Twirled in their colors and danced with a sigh.
For the goodbyes are sweet, wrapped in laughter's embrace,
With blooms filled with joy, they'll cherish the space.

Dreams Entwined in Silk

In a hall of silk petals, dreams flutter with flair,
A cosmos of laughter fills each fragrant air.
The petals wear giggles like soft, floral crowns,
And the roses regale tales of ups and downs.

"Why's the cactus so moody?" the lilies inquire,
"Because he just can't find a friend to admire!"
As laughter erupts, the gardens all sway,
With blossoms collaborating for one grand display.

In dreams entwined, they weave stories so bright,
The sunflowers twirl, entertaining the night.
"Are we weeds in disguise?" asks a bold pansy,
"Only with humor can we make it so fancy!"

With each whispered joke, their vibrant hearts soar,
For the humor in life is what flowers adore.
At the end of the day, in the twilight's soft hue,
They laugh and they dance, as fresh dreams come true.

The Cloak of Sorrowed Blooms

In a garden dressed in frowns,
Where petals dip and petals drown.
The flowers wear their tears like capes,
Pretending life is full of scrapes.

Bumblebees buzz with grumpy moans,
Dancing close to prickly thrones.
Should I water? Should I weep?
These plants have secrets they can't keep.

Underneath the sad, green shroud,
Laughter hides, a playful crowd.
A gnome trips over garden tools,
In this world where sorrow rules.

But sometimes petals laugh with glee,
Tickled by a gentle breeze.
These blooms, while cloaked in woe and gloom,
Whisper jokes about their doom.

Veils of Mourning in the Garden

In shadows draped with leafy sighs,
Sprinkled with the raindrop cries.
The weeds throw shade and gossip loud,
About the blooms that once felt proud.

A snail in black, a tiny hearse,
Moves slowly; life couldn't get worse.
While daisies giggle, rolling eyes,
As stems ruminate their goodbyes.

Each bloom waves a delicate hand,
Chasing off the gloomy band.
They wear their veils with flair anew,
And toast to all that once they knew.

With roots that dance beneath the soil,
They poke their heads, their spirits loyal.
For in this garden dressed in grief,
Lies humor, sweet, a sly relief.

A Symphony of Withered Leaves

The rustling leaves bring forth a tune,
Of weary stems beneath the moon.
As petals drop with a heavy sigh,
The wind gathers them, oh my!

Are we sad or just confused?
These blooms feel both, yet never bruised.
A concert of decay and cheer,
With crickets chirping, 'This is queer!'

A withered rose raises an old tale,
Of how she danced with a windswept gale.
While laughing weeds bend with the breeze,
Life's little jokes, a light tease.

So let's applaud those fading hues,
For every loss delivers news.
In this land of dying blooms,
The symphony of joy resumes.

Graceful Tributes to Lost Time

In a patch where laughter's wrapped in lace,
Time tiptoes by, quite out of place.
The flowers whisper tales of years,
Of puppy love and nerdy peers.

A wilting stem recalls the past,
When it stood tall, a vibrant cast.
Yet here it is, a graceful nod,
To moments spent beneath, how odd!

With bees proclaiming every wrong,
As if they'd sing an ancient song.
And every bloom, poised in delight,
Remembers sunshine, and giggles bright.

So here's to petals and each decline,
For even fading blooms can shine.
A tribute to the time once lost,
In laughter found, we pay the cost.

Shattered Silhouettes

In a garden of quirks, they stand so tall,
Flipping their petals like a gala ball.
One winked at the sun, said 'not today,'
While a bee tripped and fell in dismay.

Giggling blooms wear fancy hats,
Dancing with jests to avoid the gnats.
They puff up with pride, flaunting their flair,
While the daisies roll eyes as if to declare.

With roots tangled in gossip, they share a toast,
To the tulip's big dreams, they love to boast.
When wind blows a joke, petals all shake,
In the wildest of gardens, no one can break.

A riot of colors in a floral spree,
Laughing at blooms that take life too seriously.
With a spritz of nectar, a toast to the odd,
In this patch of petals, life's a façade.

Elegance Among Thorns

Prancing with poise, they wear sharp attire,
Fashioned in leaves that could start a fire.
A dapper cactus calls himself suave,
While dressed in a coat that's the epitome of brave.

Swanky blooms giggle at their thorny friends,
As thorns shout, 'We're tough!' till the laughter ends.
Who needs a suit when you've got a sting?
These thistles demand to be treated like kings!

In petal-board meetings, they plot and scheme,
Over afternoon tea, they're living the dream.
With puns that are sharp as their prickly side,
They laugh about elegance no one can hide.

Among graceful shadows, they strut with glee,
Sipping on nectar, as posh as can be.
With a snicker and swish, their banter ignites,
In a garden of thorns, it's all about bites.

Aritual of Blossoms

In a bloom-filled temple where petals convene,
Dancing in circles like a floral machine.
Chanting of sunshine and moisture divine,
A ritual of laughter with every design.

The daisies bring humor, the lilies their grace,
While dandelions giggle, just saving their space.
With pollen confetti, they revel in cheer,
Each bloom blooms brighter the more they adhere.

Sun-kissed and silly in soft breezy air,
Petal offerings shared, if you dare.
For when flowers unite, they turn up the fun,
In a garden of giggles, all frolics begun.

At dusk, they collapse, petals sprawled with delight,
Their beauty undimmed, like stars in the night.
With each little stem, woven stories they tell,
In a secret society, they flourish so well.

The Color of Heartache

In hues of mishap, they swirl and twine,
Petals of heartbreak, oh so divine.
A whispering breeze tells tales of despair,
While blooms wear their scars with a cheeky flare.

Violet regrets bloom with spontaneity,
Sprouting in gardens of wild hilarity.
'Love hurts!' they giggle, sassy and bold,
With roots intertwined, stories unfold.

They raise a toast to those who have stalled,
With nectar of laughter, they're never appalled.
For each thorn that pokes, there's a punchline nearby,
In the palette of woes, their joy shines a sky.

With colors so vivid, they dance and sway,
Turning heartache to humor, come what may.
In this field of folly, with petals so spry,
The heart may ache, but laughter won't die.

Botanical Mourning

In the garden where blooms once smiled,
Petals frown like a child reviled.
Ferns gossip of scents so sweet,
But daisies just shuffle their feet.

With thorns that prickle every sigh,
Even tulips seem to wonder why.
The roses roll eyes, what a scene,
As wilted blooms join in the routine.

Violets whisper secrets of dread,
While lilacs party 'round the dead.
Springtime's laughter seems out of place,
In this botanical fallen grace.

Yet in their humor, the flowers jest,
Making death feel like a light-hearted fest.
So let's toast the petals, raise a cheer,
For life, in the end, is just quite queer!

Lush Reverberations

In layers of green, a giggle we find,
Cacti chuckling, they're feeling quite blind.
Blooms bobbing heads in a tipsy display,
Are they celebrating life's wacky ballet?

The daisies form a conga line,
While orchids sip nectar, feeling divine.
Foliage flutters in the breezy shouts,
Even the weeds are dancing about.

Grapevines toss grapes in a playful fling,
While mossy mats hum a jovial swing.
Their joy in sorrow, a splendid mix,
In the lushness of loss, they play their tricks.

From ground to sky, the laughter cascades,
In botanical echoes, where light never fades.
For even in grief, there's humor to share,
In verdant parties, no moment's too rare.

Sweetness in the Sorrow

Amidst the gloom, a flower peeks,
With petals so bright, it cheekily squeaks.
Stems sway and twist in a playful dance,
Chasing the shadows, they take their chance.

Anemones giggle in the cold,
While lilies droop, feeling bold.
Forget-me-nots wink with a tease,
Turn that frown to laughter, if you please!

Though the weight of the earth may drag them low,
Each bloom has a joke ready to throw.
And in this bouquet of whimsical cheer,
Sweetness in sorrow, they'll always revere.

So let's join the frolics beneath the moon,
As flowers compose their humorous tune.
For every petal that falls like a sigh,
In bloom's witty world, we'll always comply.

The Garden of Lost Whispers

In whispers hushed, the petals converse,
With tales of old, like comedic verse.
A daffodil flirts with a bitter sweet vine,
As laughter erupts in this horticultural shrine.

The tulips gossip, slinging puns wide,
While bees snicker, caught up in their ride.
Under the moonlight, the herbs crack jokes,
Turning their tears into playful pokes.

The evening primrose winks with delight,
Mourning the moon for the joy of the night.
In the garden's embrace, laughter and tears,
Blend clumsily, dissolving our fears.

So wander we must in this fragrant sprawl,
Where even the dead have a jolly good call.
In the garden of whispers, joy does abide,
As flowers remind us, life's fun when we slide!

Petal-Soft Goodbyes

In a garden of whimsy, we wave our hands,
A flower's farewell, in silly bands.
Beneath the laughter, a soft little sigh,
As petals scatter, oh my, oh my!

Dancing on air, like a clumsy bee,
Who knew goodbyes would be so funny?
With each little shake and a floral twist,
It's hard to be sad, I must insist!

In swirls of color, we trip and we roll,
Who knew parting could tickle the soul?
A chuckle in bloom, like a joke on the vine,
So here's to the laughs, in this grand design!

As stains of laughter spill on the ground,
Petal-soft whispers of joy abound.
We wave our goodbyes with a giggly tear,
Embracing the memories, year after year!

Memories Written in Stems

In the fancy halls of floral lore,
Memories scribbled, not a bore!
With every bend of the silly roots,
We scribble our stories in leafy suits.

The daisies chuckle, the roses whine,
Telling tales over a glass of wine.
Oh, the gossip that blooms in the sun,
Each whisper a joy, each laugh a pun!

When petals unfold like letters anew,
Silly little secrets in morning dew.
In the botanical books, our tales shall soar,
Laugh-outs loud, asking for more!

With laughter entangled in vines and twines,
We plant our stories in crooked lines.
For every moment, a flower will sprout,
And in laughter's embrace, we travel about!

Mourning in Lavender Hues

In the garden of sighs, where lavender blooms,
We dance with the shadows, tapping our shoes.
Each flower's a giggle, a wink, a cheer,
Mourning's a party when friends are near!

With scents that enthrall and whispers of fun,
Sadness unwinds, like yarn from a pun.
Petals in purple, they giggle with glee,
Who knew the gray could turn into spree?

Beneath the moons and the twinkly stars,
We laugh at our hearts and the beauty in scars.
The memories linger, wrapped up in hues,
Waltzing around in our lavender shoes!

So let's toast in purple, to all that we've lost,
In laughter, we find what it truly cost.
Tears may sprinkle, but joy is the root,
In this garden of feeling, we blossom and hoot!

Garden of the Broken Heart

In a garden where giggles sprout from the ground,
The broken hearts bloom, wearing laughter all around.
With petals that tickle, and thorns that tease,
We mend our dismay, and dance with ease.

Each tear is a raindrop that nurtures the land,
Where funny little thoughts like dandelions stand.
A heart once shattered now dances so free,
In the light of the joy, we create with glee.

The daisies remind us of love that was lost,
But laughter is precious, and never the cost.
So patch up your heart with jokes and delight,
In this garden of whimsy, our spirits take flight!

With petals like pillows, we cradle our pain,
As the humor whispers, making shadows wane.
In this vast blooming playground of the smart,
We'll smile through the cracks of the broken heart!

Sorrowful Blooms

In the garden, petals sigh,
A wilted laugh that flutters by.
Pollen drips from teary eyes,
As bees buzz with awkward goodbyes.

With every gale, they cringe and shake,
A dance of sorrow, oh, for goodness' sake!
They giggle in the evening mist,
Who knew a bloom could be so trysted?

Their beauty fades, but never fears,
For every droop brings silly cheers.
The sun winks down, a jovial tease,
And ants parade with such unease.

In shadowed plots, they plot and moan,
While growing thick, they jest alone.
A garden party, who would have thought?
Sorrowful blooms, yet joyfully caught.

Gloomy Florals

In patches dark, the petals frown,
With waning hopes, they weigh them down.
A flower's joke, with roots so bleak,
Why does the sun play hide and seek?

With heavy hearts, they grasp for light,
Yet giggle softly, a comical fright.
In silken gowns, they dread the chill,
But twirl around, just for the thrill.

The wind may howl, but blooms will sway,
In skeptical play of light and gray.
Each drooping head hides a sly grin,
Playing the loss like a game they win.

So let them snicker in their gloom,
A floral comedy, they proudly bloom.
In their confessions of leafy despair,
Gloomy florals spread laughs everywhere.

Resilience in Fragility

With each soft petal, a giggle so light,
Strands of courage in a flimsy sight.
They sway in breezes, a comical dance,
In the face of a storm, they take the chance.

A two-step shuffle on fragile stems,
Creaking and laughing, their own best gems.
When rain arrives, they share a jest,
"Wet like us? Guess that's in the quest!"

Yet in their fall, they claim to rise,
For nature's folly is such a surprise.
They stash their fears beneath a petal's fold,
With a wink so bright, and a story bold.

Their resilience shines in a goofy way,
Fragile warriors in a light-hearted play.
A garden's mirth, a jubilant sight,
With every brush of the moon's soft light.

Ephemeral Grace

In fleeting moments, they make their mark,
With smiles that sparkle, igniting the dark.
A ghostly swirl of whimsy and flair,
Short-lived jokes, hanging in the air.

Petals blush as the sunlight dips,
And giggles escape from their soft-lipped quips.
A comedic fleeting, a fragrant tease,
They wink at the clock, "Do stay, if you please!"

Their grace, a wink, as they fade away,
Turning giggles to memories of play.
For what is beauty if not for laughter,
In a bountiful garden, their joy's the after.

So gather close, as they dance and twirl,
In a moment's jest, let the colors swirl.
Ephemeral, yes, but such a delight,
With every petal, they steal the night.

www.ingramcontent.com/pod-product-compliance
Lightning Source LLC
Chambersburg PA
CBHW071849160426
43209CB00003B/484